30 vegetable juices

fresh recipes for fitness, detox and raw power

Joanna Farrow

LORENZ BOOKS

This edition is published by Lorenz Books,
an imprint of Anness Publishing Ltd, Blaby Road, Wigston,
Leicestershire LE18 4SE; info@anness.com

www.lorenzbooks.com; www.annesspublishing.com

If you like the images in this book and would like to investigate
using them for publishing, promotions or advertising, please visit
our website www.practicalpictures.com for more information.

Publisher: Joanna Lorenz
Editorial Director: Helen Sudell
Consultant Editor: Catherine Stuart
Recipes: Joanna Farrow
Additional material: Suzannah Olivier
Text editor: Jenni Fleetwood
Book and jacket design: Nigel Partridge
Production Controller: Helen Wang

A CIP catalogue record for this book is available from
the British Library.

NOTES

Bracketed terms are intended for American readers.

For all recipes, quantities are given in both metric and imperial
measures and, where appropriate, in standard cups and spoons.
Follow one set of measures, but not a mixture, because
they are not interchangeable.

Standard spoon and cup measures are level.
1 tsp = 5ml, 1 tbsp = 15ml, 1 cup = 250ml/8fl oz.

Australian standard tablespoons are 20ml. Australian readers
should use 3 tsp in place of 1 tbsp for measuring small quantities.

American pints are 16fl oz/2 cups. American readers should use
20fl oz/2.5 cups in place of 1 pint when measuring liquids.

The nutritional analysis given for each recipe is calculated per
portion (i.e. serving or item), unless otherwise stated. If the recipe
gives a range, such as Serves 4–6, then the nutritional analysis will
be for the smaller portion size, i.e. 6 servings. The analysis does not
include optional ingredients, such as salt added to taste.

Medium (US large) eggs are used unless otherwise stated.

Front cover shows Basil Blush – for recipe, see page 33.

PUBLISHER'S NOTE

Contents

introduction

Juicing is an excellent way of boosting your vegetable and fruit intake and obtaining essential nutrients in a palatable and pleasurable manner. What's more – it's fun. There's something quite magical about feeding hard chunks of raw produce into a sleek machine and instantly seeing a steady stream of juice emerging from the spout. The amount of juice is surprising too. You may expect tomatoes to yield plenty of liquid, but celeriac? How can something so tough and knobbly contain so much moisture?

It's a journey of discovery. Some vegetables, especially roots, taste surprisingly sweet; others are cool and soothing, while some are bitter,

Below: Superfood broccoli is delightful in combination juices.

and best enjoyed in small portions. Most juicers – and by that we mean people, not machines – begin by using basic recipes, but rapidly invent their own combinations. Inspiration comes initially from classic concoctions like carrot and orange, or cucumber and apple, but it doesn't take long before the novice comes up with new ideas. A trip to a farmers' market might result in a shopping basket brimming with baby beetroot (beets) or new season's broad (fava) beans; the garden might yield a glut of golden courgettes (zucchini) or great handfuls of tiny tomatoes. With the best will in the world, there are only so many salads and salsas any one person can eat, but, if you add juice to the equation, nature's profligacy can be used to great effect.

Juices aren't meant to be meal replacements, except, perhaps, when an individual embarks on a detox diet for a specific period of time. Although raw fruit and vegetables can supply a lot of our dietary needs, their role should be to support a well-balanced diet. Fruit and vegetable juices provide vitamins, minerals, enzymes,

Above: Carrots are a popular base for many vegetable juices.

phytochemicals, essential fatty acids and easily assimilated carbohydrate, but they won't provide much fibre. For that, you also need to eat whole fruits and vegetables, together with pulses and other fibre-rich foods such as oats. Some people add a little of the pulp from the juice machine back into the juice, but this is not necessary if you obtain fibre in other ways. It is also essential to have sufficient protein, ideally from low fat sources such as fish, lean meat and poultry, eggs, low-fat dairy produce, pulses, seeds, nuts and grains.

When incorporating juices into your diet, many people recommend leaving at least half an hour between drinking a glass of juice and eating a meal. Starting the day with juice will benefit your digestive system and boost energy levels. If you later have a bowl of porridge or a slice of wholemeal toast topped with baked beans – foods that release energy slowly – you will function well and will not feel hungry for hours.

One of the great benefits of juicing is that it is so quick and easy – it takes a matter of minutes to produce a glass of sheer goodness. You seldom need to peel vegetables or fruit – just make sure they are clean, and free from stones or pits. Nor should you be put off by cleaning the machine. If you run a sink of soapy water before you begin, and have a bag or bin ready

Below: Celery has very few calories and the stalks can be used as stirrers.

to receive residue, you can restore your juicer to pristine cleanliness while your enjoy your juice.

Where vegetable juices score over fruit ones is that most of them are low in sugar. A typical glass of freshly squeezed orange juice can contain as much as 8 teaspoons of sugar in the form of fructose. If you were to eat the whole fruit, the fibre would slow the release of the sucrose into the bloodstream, but the fruit also impacts more rapidly on insulin levels. Root vegetables like carrots and beetroot (beets) are also high in natural sugars, but other vegetables, especially celery, cucumber and most greens, are extremely low. It has been estimated that most vegetable juices have only half as many calories as fruit juices.

Some vegetable juices do need that little bit extra, especially if your palate is accustomed to sweetness. To strike a balance, many of the vegetable juices in this book include a small amount of fruit. If you are introducing juices into your diet for the first time, or tempting children to try something new, begin with these slightly sweeter offerings, and gradually phase in pure vegetable mixtures.

Above: Add seeds such as sunflower and pumpkin for crunchy texture.

Subtler flavours can be given extra zing by the addition of herbs and spices. Ginger and chillies are especially good, and have health as well as flavour benefits.

Vegetable juices can be enjoyed throughout the day. They are better for us than tea or coffee and can even be transformed into cocktails. Wind down with a Bloody Mary, made with freshly juiced tomatoes with a dash of vodka, or try a smoothie-style blend of avocado and lime.

Vegetable juices energize, cleanse, detoxify, boost immunity and help to restore sluggish digestive tracts. Make them part of your daily diet and you'll soon see the benefits. You'll look better, feel better and have much more vitality.

essential equipment

From choosing a juicer to updating familiar kitchen items, this is what you need to begin juicing.

Centrifugal juicers
These juicers work by finely grating vegetables and fruit, and spinning them at great speed, which separates the juice from the pulp. Fibre and pulp residue are ejected into a pulp collector. Some come with a jug (pitcher) attachment that collects the juice; others require a separate jug or glass to be placed under the spout.

Masticating juices
More high-tech than centrifugal juicers, masticating juicers finely chop, rather than shred, the produce, then force the pulp through a mesh

Below: Centrifugal juicer (left) and masticating juicer.

to separate out the juice. Electric or manually operated, masticating juicers produce a greater volume of juice than centrifugal models and, because of the method of extraction, the juice contains more live enzymes.

Food processors
These multi-functional machines comprise a main bowl and a variety of attachments. For making juices and blends, the most important accessories are a strong blade that blends medium-hard or soft produce and a centrifugal juicing attachment.

Vegetable peeler
You can choose between straight blade or swivel blade.

Sharp knife
This is essential for safety as well as convenience and speed.

Chopping board
Choose a large board, and reserve it for the preparation of raw vegetables, fruits and bread.

Vegetable scrubbing brush
Handy for removing dirt from the surface of vegetables, especially roots, and an alternative to peeling.

Above: Swivel-blade peelers remove large amounts of peel in one go.

Zester
Offers a quick and mess-free way to grate rind and add citrus flavour to all kinds of juices.

Plastic spatula
Very useful for scraping residue out of a blender or food processor, without scratching the equipment.

Measuring jugs (cups)
Whether you opt for glass or plastic, choose one with the measurements clearly marked up the side.

Storage jug or vacuum flask
Once the juice has been prepared, limiting its exposure to oxygen will help to keep it for longer. Choose a jug (pitcher) with a close-fitting lid and place in the refrigerator.

buying and storing produce

The produce you use for juices should be as fresh as possible to ensure that you will get the maximum nutrients from your drinks. It is not necessary to buy vegetables that look perfect, but do avoid any that are bruised, damaged or overripe. Aim to buy produce in season if you can, to ensure your juices are bursting with health-giving vitamins and minerals.

Buy organic

There are clear advantages in choosing food grown organically. The levels of chemicals that you are exposed to via pesticides, fungicides and fertilizers will be significantly reduced, and the vegetables will often taste better because there is less water bulking out the produce. It is certainly true that if you taste an organic carrot and then compare it to

Below: Sweet dried fruit such as figs can be juiced along with vegetables.

Above: For the most flavoursome tomatoes, choose organic produce.

the taste of a non-organic carrot, the former will usually have a more solid texture and a more intense carroty flavour. This means that your blends will also have more flavour, as there is less water diluting the juice.

Useful alternatives

For convenience, and because you can't always find fresh produce out of season, it is worthwhile keeping some dried, frozen or canned vegetables to hand in your store cupboard (pantry). Use these as substitutes whenever you run out of a fresh ingredient or if you find that an ingredient is unavailable or out of season. Dried fruit can also be kept in the store cupboard. Dates, apricots and figs are particularly useful for sweetening vegetable juices.

Storing produce

All vegetables benefit from being stored in cool, dry conditions. Most should be kept in the refrigerator, but some – particularly the vegetable fruits, such as tomatoes and peppers – will be fine for a few days at room temperature unless they are very ripe and soft (in which case, refrigerate immediately and use as soon as possible). Onions, on the other hand, are best kept out of the refrigerator, as they benefit from free air circulation. Otherwise they are likely to rot.

Whole nuts and seeds and dry ingredients such as wheatgerm should be kept in airtight jars or packets in the refrigerator. They will usually keep for about a month.

Below: Store different types of vegetables separately to preserve their freshness.

juicing and blending techniques

Once you have purchased the necessary equipment for juicing or blending you will want to get started as soon as possible. For maximum freshness and flavour, prepare the vegetables just before you are ready to juice them. There are slightly different requirements for preparing produce for each type of machine. Always read the equipment manufacturer's instructions first.

Using centrifugal and masticating juicers

Although centrifugal and masticating juicers function in different ways, the preparation of produce and the basic principles for using the machines are much the same. Choose firm produce, and remember that most vegetables do not need to be peeled before use. However, large stones (pits) of vegetable fruits such as avocados will need to be removed.

1 Scrub any vegetables that you are not going to peel with a hard brush under cold running water to get rid of dirt. If there is a waxy residue, then use a little bit of soap or washing-up liquid (dishwashing detergent) to help dissolve this, then rinse the produce thoroughly under cold running water.

2 To remove a large pit (stone), cut round the middle of the fruit, using a small, sharp knife, then twist to break into two halves. Strike the stone to pierce it, and lift it away.

3 All leafy vegetables, such as cabbages, lettuce and spinach, can be put through a juicer. Include the outer leaves, which are nutritionally superior, although these must be washed thoroughly first.

4 When pushing the produce through the feeder tube of the machine, it is very important that you use the

plunger provided. Remember to position a jug (pitcher) or glass under the nozzle of the machine to catch the juice, otherwise it will spray all over the work surface.

5 Put the ingredients through the machine in manageable quantities. Cut larger vegetables into quarters, for example, and alternate them if possible to ensure that the juices mix well. If you push too many pieces of fruit or vegetable through in one go, or push through pieces that are too large, the machine will clog up.

Cook's tip

When juicing a range of vegetables, push a hard ingredient, such as a carrot, through after softer ingredients, such as cabbage. This will keep the juice flowing freely and will prevent blockages. If the vegetable is quite long, keep pushing through until the tip is about to disappear.

Cleaning juicers, blenders and food processors

The one and only dreary thing about making juices and blends is that the equipment needs to be cleaned soon afterwards. However, there are some simple, no-fuss ways of making this chore much easier.

Cleaning a juicer, blender or food processor thoroughly is important if you want to avoid unhealthy bacteria, and the best time to do this is straight after you have made the juice or smoothie and poured it into glasses or a jug (pitcher). If you clean the parts of a juicer, blender or food processor immediately (or at least put them in to soak), the pulp and residue should just rinse off easily. Take great care when handling detachable blades – it is better not to leave these immersed in the water for safety reasons.

1 To clean a centrifugal or masticating juicer, or food processor, fill a sink with cold water and take the equipment apart, following the manufacturer's instructions.

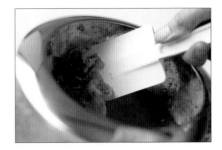

2 Using a plastic spatula or spoon, scoop off any large pieces of residue (such as the fruit and vegetable pulp that collects inside the spout of the juicer or around the blades) and discard it. Better still, add to a compost heap in the garden.

3 Plunge the non-electrical, removable machine parts of the juicer or food processor into the sink full of cold water and leave them to soak until you are ready to clean them – this will probably be after you've sat back and enjoyed your freshly made juice or blend. Soaking the machine parts will help to loosen any remaining fruit and vegetable pulp and will make cleaning them much easier.

4 After soaking, either carefully handwash the non-electrical, removable machine parts or put them into a dishwasher on a normal setting.

5 Scrub any attachments that you have used with a firm brush to loosen any residue that is still clinging. Always take care when handling grating attachments as they are extremely sharp.

6 The removable components of your juicer, blender or food processor may become stained, especially if using vibrantly coloured ingredients. Soak stained components every now and then in plenty of cold water with a little bleach added. Be sure to rinse the parts thoroughly afterwards, then allow to dry before reassembling.

Cook's tip

Strongly flavoured vegetables such as onion and garlic tend to cling to machinery, so running half a lemon through the machine can help to mop up powerful scents.

root and tuber vegetables

Carrot is the only root vegetable that is suitable to be used as a base juice, but others can be included in smaller proportions in juices and blends. Root vegetables store best in cool, dry conditions, although beetroot (beet) is best kept in the refrigerator.

Preparing roots and tubers

You do not usually need to peel carrots, beetroot (beet), celeriac, parsnips, radishes, swedes (rutabagas), turnips, sweet potatoes or yams. While you can include potato skin, you must be sure to cut away any peel or flesh that is sprouting or green in any way. This green colour indicates the presence of a highly toxic alkaloid called solanine, which could cause illness.

Below: Beetroot should be juiced raw, and can be scrubbed rather than peeled. It contributes a rich red colour.

Above: If leaving the skin on roots and tubers, scrub them well before juicing.

Juicing roots and tubers

When root vegetables are juiced they tend to produce foam, which settles at the top of the juice. This can taste a bit earthy even when the vegetables have been scrubbed clean. However, this taste indicates their high mineral content so the topping should be drunk for maximum benefit (you can mix it in with the rest of the juice).

Juicing properties

Carrot: Naturally sweet juice can be used as a base. There is no need to peel them unless using very old carrots.

Right: Sweet baby carrots make particularly delicious juices.

Beetroot (beet): Always juice raw. Juice is strong-tasting, so use about one-quarter beetroot juice to three-quarters other juice.
Parsnip: Sweet, creamy juice. Use in smaller quantities than carrot juice – about one-quarter parsnip to three-quarters other juice. Works well with leafy, peppery vegetables.
Radish: Strong peppery taste; use in small quantities to boost flavour.
Sweet potatoes and yams: Vary in colour. Choose unblemished, smooth produce and store in a dark, cool, dry place.
Celeriac, swedes and turnips: These work best when added to other vegetable blends such as carrot-based or leafy green juices.
Potatoes: Always use raw, and in small amounts. Nutty flavour works well with other vegetables.

leafy and brassica vegetables

The brassica family includes broccoli, cauliflower and brussels sprouts. Ideally these, and all leafy vegetables, should be stored in the refrigerator to avoid wilting, yellowing or browning, and they are best used as soon as possible after purchase as they quickly lose their nutritional value. Generally you will add one-quarter juice made from green leaves to three-quarters juice made from other ingredients.

Left and below: Kale contributes a peppery kick to vegetable juices, while brussels sprouts add a mild and pleasant nutty flavour. Both are useful sources of vitamin C.

Loose, leafy vegetables

Separate out the leaves and wash thoroughly. Cut away any that are discoloured but keep the outer leaves as they are richer in nutrients than the interior ones. Do not discard the cores of lettuce or any leaf stems, so that they can be safely juiced.

Below: Separate out the leaves of vegetables such as spinach to wash.

Tightly packed leaves

Vegetables such as chicory (Belgian endive) or Chinese leaves (Chinese cabbage) should be washed, then quartered or chopped into an appropriate size to pass through the neck of the machine. Cut broccoli and cauliflower into florets and wash the pieces thoroughly. The cores can also be juiced.

Juicing leafy and brassica vegetables

To extract the maximum juice it is best to alternate putting leaves through the juicer with a hard vegetable or fruit such as carrot or apple. This keeps the machine working efficiently.

Juicing properties

Cabbages and brussels sprouts: Either red or green cabbage can be juiced. Both contribute a surprisingly light taste so long as the quantity used does not overwhelm the blend. About one-eighth to one-quarter cabbage is the right quantity in any juice. Brussels sprouts, which are really just mini-cabbages, should be treated in the same way. Both work well when combined with sweeter fruit bases.

Spinach: Mild, slightly peppery taste; like cabbage, it is best used in small quantities with sweeter bases.

Cauliflower and Broccoli: The effects of juicing these are quite different: broccoli tastes slightly bitter while cauliflower is creamy. They are best used in small quantities with other milder flavours such as carrot or beetroot (beet).

Lettuce, watercress and kale: Use in small quantities and with other blends.

vegetable fruits

Some vegetables are actually the fruit of the plant, although they are not sweet in the way that we usually think of fruit. If allowed to ripen on the plant they are all exceptionally rich in various nutrients.

Preparing vegetable fruits

Some vegetable fruits, like (bell) peppers, are very straightforward to prepare. Simply cut in half lengthways, cut away the stem, seeds and pith, and wash under running water before juicing.

Avocado requires a little more work. Cut in half lengthways, ease the two halves apart and impale the stone (pit) on the knife or scoop it out with a spoon. Scoop out the flesh and place it in a blender or food

Below: (Bell) peppers can be prepared for juicing in no time at all. All you need is a sharp knife.

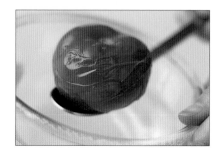

Above: The trick with skinning tomatoes is to leave them in hot water just long enough for the skin to split.

processor with other ingredients. (Avocados are too soft to put in a juicer.) You could also mash the flesh using a fork and stir it in by hand.

Tomatoes can be juiced whole or skinned first. To skin tomatoes, place them in a heatproof bowl and pour boiling water over them. Leave to soak for 2–3 minutes. Lift the tomatoes out, nick the skin with the point of a knife and it should begin to peel back. Peel off the loosened skin before juicing the flesh.

Juicing properties

Avocado: When properly ripe, these are rich and slightly nutty tasting. They lend a creamy texture to juices and can be used to thicken a blend as an alternative to milk. They combine well with most vegetable juices – adding a little lemon juice will help cut through the richness and will also slow down any discoloration.

Peppers: Although they come in a variety of colours, (bell) peppers are, in fact, all the same vegetable – green peppers are simply unripe red peppers. The taste of yellow, orange and red peppers is similarly sweet, while green ones have a slightly more bitter flavour. Peppers can dominate a juice and so are best used in small quantities. They are ideal combined with tomato juice.

Tomatoes: Sweet when ripe and acidic when unripe. Select vine-ripened tomatoes for the best flavour. Tomatoes mix well with most other vegetables and fruits. They are often used as a base juice. Recent research suggests that tomatoes may be an important cancer-fighting food.

Above: Avocados help to thicken the texture of juices.

squash vegetables

The high water content of these vegetables makes them ideal for juicing in a centrifugal or masticating juicer. Cucumbers are available all year round and the best variety to use for juicing is the European (hothouse) cucumber. Courgettes (zucchini) are also available all year round, but are at their best in the summer, and other squashes only appear in the autumn (fall).

Cucumbers and courgettes should be stored in the refrigerator, but squashes like butternut squash and pumpkin may be kept for up to a week or two in cool, dry conditions.

Preparing squash vegetables
Cucumbers and courgettes can be prepared by washing the skin, using a scrubbing brush if the vegetables are

Below: It is not essential to peel courgettes (zucchini) before juicing.

Above: Cooling cucumbers are often juiced in hot countries.

waxed. Cut into large chunks and push through the juicer. You could also blend cucumbers in a blender or food processor as they contain such a high percentage of water.

Prepare larger squashes, such as butternut and pumpkin, by using a very sharp knife to cut them in half and scoop out most of the seeds, leaving some to go through the juicer, if you like. Slice away the peel, then cut the flesh into large chunks and push through the juicer with the aid of a plunger.

Right: Despite their firm flesh, larger squash vegetables such as pumpkin will juice easily and combine well with sweeter vegetables.

Juicing properties
Cucumbers and courgette (zucchini): When juiced, all cucumbers are mild and tasty, although small cucumbers have the best flavour. Ideal for using as a base juice, they mix well with both vegetables and fruit. Courgettes are similar to cucumbers when juiced, but not quite as sweet.

Pumpkins and butternut squash: Both of these squashes produce a juice with a surprisingly sweet and nutty taste, but it is not a juice that you would want to drink on its own. Mix one-quarter pumpkin or squash juice with three-quarters other juice such as carrot or cucumber, along with something else to give it a bit of zing – perhaps an onion. Cinnamon, ginger, allspice or nutmeg can be added to smooth, savoury-sweet blends.

pod, shoot and bulb vegetables

All of these vegetables need to be put through a juicer. They all produce fairly strong tasting juices which should be combined with other vegetables.

Preparing pod, shoot and bulb vegetables

Pod vegetables such as French (green) beans, broad (fava) beans, runner (green) beans and mangetout (snow peas) do not need any preparation other than ensuring that they are clean. They do not require stringing or trimming as the juicer will simply turn the undesirable parts of the vegetables into pulp.

To prepare bulb vegetables, pull off the outer leaves and wash these vegetables thoroughly before juicing, then cut into chunks the right size for

Below: Rich in vitamins, asparagus gives the ultimate health kick, but should always be juiced with other vegetables.

your machine. It is not essential to remove the outer leaves or skin from onions, spring onions (scallions), leeks, fennel and celery, but they must be washed thoroughly.

Except for globe artichokes, all shoot vegetables can simply be cleaned and juiced as they are. For alfalfa and cress, this will probably mean cutting the shoots from the root as the roots are likely to be embedded in soil. You will need to alternate shoot vegetables with hard vegetables, such as carrots, otherwise no juice will come out.

To prepare globe artichokes, remove the woody stem, then cut the rest of the flower into chunks and push through the juicer.

Juicing properties

Beans and mangetout: Choose firm, crisp beans for the best results – choices include broad (fava), runner (green) and French (green) beans. Avoid any beans that have been pre-trimmed or that are going soft.

With the exception of mangetout (snow peas), which make a fairly mild and sweet juice, beans do not taste great when juiced, so mix them with other vegetables for a balanced flavour.

Above: Prepare globe artichokes by removing the woody stem, then cutting into chunks before juicing.

Fennel and celery: Use firm, pale green produce. Fennel tastes of aniseed, and juiced celery, when combined, does not taste nearly as strong as the raw vegetable. Combine with carrot, apple or pear, at a ratio of about one-fifth fennel or celery to four-fifths other juice.

Onions and leeks: All onions, including shallots, spring onions (scallions) and even red (Italian) onions, produce strong-tasting juices. You only need to add a tiny quantity to a general vegetable juice. Leek juice is not as strong as onion juice.

Asparagus: Juice is best combined with other vegetables.

Beansprouts, cress and alfalfa: All give fairly strong, peppery juices, so need to be mixed with other vegetable juices.

herbs, spices and supplements

Vegetable juices are, by nature, simple and convenient, and some are best served with no greater addition than crushed ice. However, a shot of citrus juice, a sprinking of chopped herbs or chilli, a touch of spice or a dash of natural sweetness can really lift the flavour of a juice, as well as boosting energy and health.

Fresh herbs

Leafy herbs such as parsley, coriander (cilantro) and tarragon blend beautifully with vegetables, although they should always be put through a juicer with hard ingredients, such as carrots, so that the machine does not become clogged. Many herbs have excellent health properties too, and have been used for centuries to help to relieve conditions ranging from headache to indigestion.

Below: Root ginger adds heat and flavour to a variety of juices.

Above: Use herbs such as tarragon to add fresh flavour to vegetable juices.

Spices

These can be used in subtle amounts to boost flavour. Root ginger complements many vegetable juices, particularly sweeter blends using beetroot (beet), carrot, butternut squash, or a mixture of vegetables and fruits. It is a warming, pungent spice, and should be added in moderation so as not to overpower.

Chilli, also renowned for its fiery properties, is an excellent energizer. It is often used in small quantities in more complex vegetable blends using several main ingredients. Chilli juice tends to cling to metal machinery parts, so chillies should be ground and added separately.

Ground spices such as cumin (for nutty, savoury blends) and nutmeg or cinnamon (for sweeter blends

such as carrot or butternut squash) score highly on convenience, as do ready-made sauces such as Tabasco, sweet chilli or creamed horseradish. If you prefer, substitute the latter with the ground natural root, although, like chilli, it should not be put through a juicer but be prepared separately.

Other flavourings and supplements

Seeds, such as pumpkin and linseeds (flax seeds), are renowned superfoods and excellent for texture. Chop them roughly before putting through the juicer. Wheatgrass — an excellent detoxifier — has a distinctive flavour and works well with otherwise bland blends. Powdered medicinal plants and herbs such as kelp, ginseng and echinacea are often added for all-round repair and vitality.

Below: Chillies are best ground and added separately to juices as their juice would cling to machinery.

breakfast blends

clean sweep

This juice is so packed with goodness, you can almost feel it cleansing and detoxing your body. As well as valuable vitamins, the carrots and grapes provide plenty of natural sweetness, which blends perfectly with the mild pepperiness of the celery and fresh scent of parsley. Drink this juice on a regular basis to give your system a thorough clean-out.

Makes 1 tall glass

2 celery sticks
300g/11oz carrots
150g/5oz green
   grapes

several large sprigs of
   parsley
celery or carrot sticks,
   to serve

1 Using a sharp knife, roughly chop 1 celery stick and all the carrots. Push half of the celery and half of the carrots through a juicer, then add half the grapes and the parsley sprigs.

2 Add the remaining celery, carrots and grapes in the same way and juice until combined. Place some ice cubes in a tall glass and pour over the juice, using a celery or carrot stick as a stirrer.

Energy 99kcal/417kJ; Protein 1.3g; Carbohydrate 23.6g, of which sugars 22.8g; Fat 0.6g, of which saturates 0.2g; Cholesterol 0mg; Calcium 54mg; Fibre 1.3g; Sodium 48mg.

carrot and ginger juice

Fresh root ginger is one of the best natural cures for indigestion and it helps to settle upset stomachs, whether caused by food poisoning or motion sickness. In this unusual fruity blend, it is simply mixed with sweet-tasting carrot and fresh, juicy pineapple, creating a quick and easy remedy that can be juiced up in minutes – and tastes delicious too.

Makes 1 glass

1 carrot
1/2 small pineapple
25g/1oz fresh root ginger
ice cubes

Cook's tip
Before preparing the pineapple, turn it upside down and leave for half an hour – this makes it juicier.

1 Chop the carrot roughly. Using a sharp knife, cut away the skin from the pineapple, then halve and remove the core. Roughly slice the pineapple flesh. Peel and roughly chop the ginger.

2 Push the sliced pineapple through the juicer first, followed by the chopped carrot and ginger. When combined, pour into a glass. Add a handful of ice cubes and serve immediately.

Energy 108kcal/461kJ; Protein 1.3g; Carbohydrate 26.1g, of which sugars 25.8g; Fat 0.6g, of which saturates 0.1g; Cholesterol 0mg; Calcium 55mg; Fibre 4.2g; Sodium 23mg.

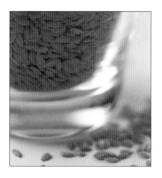

vitality juice

This nutritious blend of ripe, juicy fruit, wheatgerm, yogurt, seeds and watercress makes a great-tasting tonic. If you would prefer, use yogurt made from goat's milk, sheep's milk or soya. There is the ideal solution for those who never have time for breakfast in the morning – a perfectly portable energy kick that can be enjoyed en route to your destination!

Makes 1 tall glass or 2 small glasses

25g/1oz watercress
1 large ripe pear
30ml/2 tbsp wheatgerm
150ml/¼ pint/⅔ cup
    natural (plain) yogurt
15ml/1 tbsp linseeds
    (flax seeds)
10ml/2 tbsp lemon juice
mineral water (optional)
ice cubes

1 Roughly chop the watercress (you do not need to remove the tough stalks). Peel, core and chop the pear.

2 Put the watercress and pear in a blender or food processor with the wheatgerm and blend until smooth. Use a plastic spatula to scrape the mixture down from the side of the bowl, if necessary.

3 Add the yogurt, seeds and lemon juice to the blender or food processor and blend until evenly combined.

4 Thin with a little mineral water if the mixture is too thick and pour over ice cubes in one tall glass or two small ones. Decorate with a sprig or two of the remaining watercress, if you like.

Health tips
• When juicing leafy vegetables and herbs, retain the stalks because this is where the nutrients are concentrated. They go through the juicer really easily, too.
• Fresh pears are a great energizer and can help give you a kick-start in the morning if you have a long, busy day ahead or a deadline to meet.

Energy 346kcal/1454kJ; Protein 19.6g; Carbohydrate 39.9g, of which sugars 31.2g; Fat 13.4g, of which saturates 2.5g; Cholesterol 2mg; Calcium 461mg; Fibre 3.5g; Sodium 146mg.

morning after

A Bloody Mary is a traditional hangover cure with a solid reputation for actually working. Spicy, refreshing and mildly alcoholic – if you can face the vodka – this version will invigorate sluggish energy levels with a generous dose of vitamin C and antioxidants to cleanse your system, and help you face the day ahead.

Makes 1 large glass

300g/11oz ripe tomatoes
5ml/1 tsp Tabasco or
 Worcestershire sauce
5ml/1 tsp lemon juice
15–30ml/1–2 tbsp vodka
 (optional)
crushed ice
celery leaves, to decorate

1 Roughly chop the tomatoes and blend in a food processor or blender.

Cook's tip
If you prefer, simply push the chopped tomatoes through a sieve rather than juicing them.

2 Add the Tabasco or Worcestershire sauce and lemon juice to the tomato juice, with the vodka if using. Pour over plenty of crushed ice in a tall glass. Decorate with a few celery leaves and serve.

Energy 54kcal/233kJ; Protein 2.2g; Carbohydrate 10.1g, of which sugars 10g; Fat 0.9g, of which saturates 0.3g; Cholesterol 0mg; Calcium 31mg; Fibre 3g; Sodium 87mg.

wheatgrass tonic

The nutritional benefits of wheatgrass are enormous. It is grown from wheat berries and is a concentrated source of chlorophyll, which combats tiredness, and it also provides enzymes, vitamins and minerals. It has a distinctive flavour so in this juice it is blended with mild white cabbage, but it is just as tasty combined with other vegetables instead.

Makes 1 small glass

50g/2oz white cabbage
90g/3¹/₂oz wheatgrass

Cook's tip
Wheatgrass is best prepared in a masticating juicer as it is so fibrous.

1 Using a small, sharp knife, roughly shred the cabbage.

2 Push the shredded cabbage through a juicer, alternating it with the wheatgrass.

3 Pour the juice into a small glass and serve immediately.

Variation
You can add half a cucumber or an apple to make a longer drink. Pear also blends in well.

Energy 36kcal/149kJ; Protein 3.2g; Carbohydrate 3.9g, of which sugars 3.8g; Fat 0.8g, of which saturates 0.1g; Cholesterol 0mg; Calcium 178mg; Fibre 1.9g; Sodium 130mg.

bean good

Beansprouts are a highly nutritious food, bursting with vitamins B and C. You can even sprout your own quite easily for a regular, fresh supply. Although mild in flavour, their juiciness works well in any nourishing blend. Mixed with broccoli, another superfood, and naturally sweet fruits, this blend is a real tonic for your skin and hair.

Makes 1 tall glass or 2 small glasses

90g/3¹/₂oz broccoli
1 large pear
90g/3¹/₂oz/scant ¹/₂ cup beansprouts
200g/7oz green grapes
ice cubes and sliced green grapes

1 Using a small, sharp knife, cut the broccoli into pieces small enough to fit through a juicer funnel.

2 Quarter the pear and carefully remove the core, then roughly chop the flesh into small chunks.

3 Push all the ingredients through the juicer. Pour into 1 tall glass or 2 small glasses and serve with ice cubes and sliced green grapes.

Cook's tip
To sprout your own beansprouts, place 50g/2oz dried sprouting beans in a large-rimmed jar, and fill to halfway with water. Secure a piece of muslin (cheesecloth) over the top of the jar and leave to stand overnight. Drain, rinse, and drain again the next day.

Energy 119kcal/505kJ; Protein 3.9g; Carbohydrate 25.5g, of which sugars 24.6g; Fat 0.8g, of which saturates 0.2g; Cholesterol 0mg; Calcium 56mg; Fibre 2.2g; Sodium 10mg.

bright eyes

This vibrant, intensely flavoured carrot and clementine combination is packed with vitamin A, which is essential for healthy vision, and vitamin C to give an extra boost to the whole system. Thin-skinned citrus fruits like clementines can be put through the juicer without peeling, adding a zesty kick to the final mix — and saving time when you're in a hurry.

Makes 2 tall glasses

200g/7oz carrots
6 clementines, plus extra wedges or slices to decorate
ice cubes

1 Scrub the carrots and, using a sharp knife, chop them into large chunks of a similar size. Quarter the clementines, discarding any pips (seeds).

2 Push the clementine quarters through a juicer, then repeat the procedure with the carrot chunks.

3 Pour the juice over ice cubes in tall glasses and decorate each glass with a wedge or slice of clementine, if you like.

Cook's tip
Take the tingle factor up a notch and add some extra zing by spicing up the mix a little. Peel and slice some fresh root ginger and push through the juicer with the clementines and carrots.

Energy 71kcal/299kJ; Protein 1.6g; Carbohydrate 16.4g, of which sugars 16g; Fat 0.4g, of which saturates 0.1g; Cholesterol 0mg; Calcium 56mg; Fibre 3.3g; Sodium 24mg.

apple and leaf lift-off

Makes 1 tall glass

1 apple
150g/5oz green grapes
small handful of fresh
   coriander (cilantro),
   stalks included
25g/1oz watercress or
   rocket (arugula)
15ml/1 tbsp freshly
   squeezed lime juice

This wonderful blend of fresh leaves, apple, grapes and lime juice is the perfect rejuvenator and is great for treating skin, liver and kidney disorders. Use any type of apple; most juice well.

1 Using a sharp knife, quarter the apple. Using a juicer, juice the apple and grapes, followed by the coriander and the watercress or rocket.

2 Add the lime juice to the fruit and herb mixture and stir well. Pour the mixture into a tall glass and serve.

Cook's tip
Apples will combine well with many vegetables, so it's worth keeping a big bag in the kitchen.

Energy 135kcal/581kJ; Protein 3.8g; Carbohydrate 29.5g, of which sugars 29.5g; Fat 1.2g, of which saturates 0.3g; Cholesterol 0mg; Calcium 192mg; Fibre 3.6g; Sodium 53mg.

fennel fusion

This hefty combination of raw vegetables and apples makes a surprisingly delicious juice – fresh fennel has a distinctive aniseed flavour that blends well with both fruit and vegetables. Cabbage has natural anti-bacterial properties, while apples and fennel can help to cleanse the system. As an alternative, use two or three sticks of celery instead of the fennel.

Makes 1 tall glass

1/2 small red cabbage
1/2 fennel bulb
2 apples
15ml/1 tbsp lemon juice

1 Roughly slice the cabbage and fennel and quarter the apples. Using a juicer, juice the vegetables and fruit in mixed batches.

2 Add the lemon juice to the juice mixture and stir. Pour into a glass and serve immediately.

Cook's tip
Buy really firm, fresh-looking fennel. If left on the supermarket shelves, it quickly discolours and turns fibrous.

Energy 183kcal/779kJ; Protein 5.5g; Carbohydrate 40.3g, of which sugars 39.9g; Fat 1.1g, of which saturates 0g; Cholesterol 0mg; Calcium 158mg; Fibre 2.8g; Sodium 42mg.

iron energizer

50g/2oz/¹/₄ cup ready-
  to-eat dried apricots
15ml/1 tbsp pumpkin
  seeds
250g/9oz carrots
50g/2oz spinach
15ml/1 tbsp lemon juice
10ml/2 tsp kelp powder
mineral water
spinach leaf and pumpkin
  seeds, to decorate

This energizing drink contains spinach, apricots, carrots and pumpkin seeds, which are all rich in iron, as well as kelp, a type of seaweed, to give you an invigorating lift.

1 Chop the apricots finely, cover with 100ml/3¹/₂ fl oz/ scant ¹/₂ cup boiling water and leave for 10 minutes. Meanwhile, chop the pumpkin seeds and roughly chop the carrots.

2 Drain the apricots. Push the spinach through a juicer, followed by the apricots and carrots.

3 Stir in the lemon juice, chopped pumpkin seeds and kelp powder.

4 Pour the juice into a glass, top up with a little mineral water, decorate with a spinach leaf and pumpkin seeds, then serve immediately.

Energy 266kcal/1115kJ; Protein 7.9g; Carbohydrate 41.6g, of which sugars 37.8g; Fat 8.6g, of which saturates 1g; Cholesterol 0mg; Calcium 201mg; Fibre 4.1g; Sodium 140mg.

body builder

The slightly bitter flavour of chicory is balanced by the sweet banana in this healthy drink.

115g/4oz chicory (Belgian
  endive), chopped
30ml/2 tbsp wheatgerm
1 large banana, chopped
130g/4¹/₂oz/generous
  ¹/₂ cup soya yogurt
30ml/2 tbsp linseeds
  (flax seeds)
juice of 1 lime
juice of 1 large orange
mineral water (optional)
linseeds and grated lime
  rind, to decorate

Cook's tips
• Linseeds (flax seeds) are a good source of omega 3 and omega 6 essential fatty acids.
• Wheatgerm is packed with B and E vitamins.

1 Put the chicory, wheatgerm, two-thirds of the banana, the yogurt and linseeds in a blender or food processor. Blend until smooth, then, using a plastic spatula or spoon, scrape down the side of the bowl.

2 Add the lime and orange juice to the yogurt mixture and blend. Pour the juice into a large glass and top up with mineral water. Decorate with linseeds, lime rind and the remaining banana, then serve.

Energy 384kcal/1619kJ; Protein 18.4g; Carbohydrate 41.6g, of which sugars 31.1g; Fat 14.1g, of which saturates 2.5g; Cholesterol 3mg; Calcium 127mg; Fibre 4.8g; Sodium 10mg.

daytime
boosters

parsnip pep

Although parsnips yield a relatively small amount of juice, the juicer produces an amazingly thick, sweet and creamy drink, perfect for adding body to any raw fruit and vegetable blend. Refreshing fennel, apple and pear are the perfect foils for the intense sweetness of parsnip and together produce the most wonderful power-pack of a fresh juice.

Makes 2 small glasses

115g/4oz fennel
200g/7oz parsnips
1 apple
1 pear
small handful of flat leaf
    parsley
crushed ice

Cook's tip
Parsnips are at their sweetest a few weeks after the first frost of late autumn (fall) so try a shot of this wonderful juice when you are most in need of a little winter boost. With its mild, sweet flavour, this is a good drink for children, or anyone new to juicing.

1 Cut the fennel and parsnips into large similar-size chunks. Quarter the apple and pear, carefully removing the core, if you like, then cut the quartered pieces in half.

2 Push half the prepared fruit and vegetables through a juicer, then follow with the parsley and the remaining fruit and vegetables.

3 Fill small glasses with ice and pour the juice over. Serve immediately.

Energy 113kcal/477kJ; Protein 2.7g; Carbohydrate 24g, of which sugars 17.2g; Fat 1.3g, of which saturates 0.2g; Cholesterol 0mg; Calcium 65mg; Fibre 2.2g; Sodium 19mg.

basil blush

Some herbs just don't juice well, losing their aromatic flavour and turning muddy and dull. Basil, however, is an excellent juicer, keeping its distinctive fresh fragrance. It makes the perfect partner for mild, refreshing cucumber and the ripest, juiciest tomatoes you can find. Choose the freshest vegetables around, preferably from your own garden.

Makes 1–2 small glasses

1/2 cucumber, peeled
a handful of fresh basil, plus extra to decorate
350g/12oz tomatoes
ice cubes

1 Quarter the cucumber lengthways – do not remove the seeds. Push the tomatoes through a juicer with the basil, then do the same with the cucumber.

2 Pour the blended tomato, basil and cucumber juice over cubes of ice in one or two glasses and serve decorated with a few fresh sprigs of basil.

Cook's tips
• You don't have to peel the cucumber, but the juice will have a fresher, lighter colour without the peel.
• Grow your own basil in a pot on a sunny window ledge or a tub on the patio and you'll always have fresh leaves for recipes like this.

Energy 40kcal/168kJ; Protein 1.9g; Carbohydrate 7g, of which sugars 6.8g; Fat 0.7g, of which saturates 0.2g; Cholesterol 0mg; Calcium 31mg; Fibre 2.4g; Sodium 19mg.

ginseng juice

Ginseng is a natural cure-all that is claimed to stimulate digestion, reduce tiredness, alleviate stress, strengthen the immune system and even revive a flagging libido. Here it is added to the juice as a powder.

Makes 1 tall glass

1 red (bell) pepper
200g/7oz pumpkin
1 large apricot
squeeze of lemon juice
5ml/1 tsp ginseng
   powder
ice cubes (optional)

1 Using a sharp knife, discard the core from the pepper and roughly chop the flesh. Slice the pumpkin in half. Scoop out the seeds and then cut away the skin. Chop the flesh. Halve and stone (pit) the apricot.

2 Push the pumpkin, pepper and apricot pieces through a juicer. Add a squeeze of lemon juice and the ginseng powder, and stir well to mix together. Pour the juice over ice cubes in a tall glass and serve.

Energy 94kcal/398kJ; Protein 3.5g; Carbohydrate 18.5g, of which sugars 17g; Fat 1.1g, of which saturates 0.4g; Cholesterol 0mg; Calcium 78mg; Fibre 5.5g; Sodium 8mg.

immune zoom

Red- and orange-coloured vegetables and fruits are particularly good for fighting off colds or flu, and are full of powerful antioxidants.

Makes 2 glasses

1 small mango
1 carrot
2 passion fruit
juice of 1 orange
5ml/1 tsp echinacea
mineral water (optional)
ice cubes (optional)

1 Halve the mango, cutting down one side of the flat stone (pit). Remove the stone, scoop the flesh from the skin, roughly chop and push through the juicer.

2 Roughly chop the carrot. Halve the passion fruit, scoop out the pulp and put it into the juicer, followed by the chopped carrot. Add the orange juice and echinacea, then blend briefly.

3 If you like, thin with a little mineral water, then pour over ice cubes into two glasses and serve immediately. Otherwise, transfer the juice into a jug (pitcher) and chill in the refrigerator, then serve with slices of mango.

Energy 69kcal/296kJ; Protein 1.2g; Carbohydrate 16.7g, of which sugars 16.4g; Fat 0.3g, of which saturates 0.1g; Cholesterol 0mg; Calcium 15mg; Fibre 0.5g; Sodium 8mg.

veggie boost

This simple blend makes a great juice boost. It has pure clean flavours and a chilli kick that is guaranteed to revitalize flagging energy levels. Tomatoes and carrots are rich in the valuable antioxidant betacarotene, which is reputed to fight cancer, and they contain a good supply of vitamins A, C and E, all of which are essential for good health.

Makes 2 small glasses

3 tomatoes
1 fresh red or green chilli
250g/9oz carrots
juice of 1 orange
crushed ice

Cook's tips
• Non-organic carrots may contain a lot of chemicals in their skins, so, if using, you should scrub them well or peel before use.
• Chilli juice tends to linger on the macerating plate of a juicer, so you may prefer to chop it finely by hand and add to the finished juice, or omit and add a dash of Tabasco sauce instead.

1 Quarter the tomatoes and chop the chilli. (If you prefer a milder juice, remove the seeds and white pith from the chilli before chopping.) Scrub the carrots and chop them roughly.

2 Push the tomato and chilli through a juicer, then follow with the carrots. Add the orange juice and stir well to mix. Fill two tumblers with crushed ice, pour the juice over and serve.

Energy 84kcal/351kJ; Protein 2.7g; Carbohydrate 16.9g, of which sugars 16.3g; Fat 1g, of which saturates 0.3g; Cholesterol 0mg; Calcium 52mg; Fibre 4.6g; Sodium 49mg.

ruby roots

Beetroot has the highest sugar content of any vegetable and, not surprisingly, makes one of the most delicious, sweet juices, with a vibrant red colour and a rich yet refreshing taste. Despite its firm texture, beetroot can be juiced raw and its intense flavour combines wonderfully with tangy citrus fruits and fresh root ginger. Enjoy this juice as a natural cleanser.

1 Scrub the beetroot, then trim and cut it into quarters. Push half through a juicer, followed by the ginger and remaining beetroot.

2 Squeeze the juice from the orange and add to the beetroot juice.

3 Place the ice cubes in a glass or clear glass cup. Pour the blended juice over the top and serve immediately.

Makes 1 glass

200g/7oz raw beetroot (beets)
1cm/½in piece fresh root ginger, peeled
1 large orange
ice cubes

Cook's tip
Blood-red beetroot produces an intense, jewel-coloured juice that is packed with vitamins and minerals, making it the perfect tonic and the ultimate health juice.

Energy 90kcal/385kJ; Protein 3.6g; Carbohydrate 19.6g, of which sugars 18.4g; Fat 0.3g, of which saturates 0g; Cholesterol 0mg; Calcium 45mg; Fibre 3.8g; Sodium 137mg.

Gazpacho juice

Inspired by the classic Spanish soup, this fabulous juice looks and tastes delicious. Fresh salad vegetables can be thrown into a blender or food processor and whizzed up in moments to create a refreshing, invigorating drink.

Makes 4–5 glasses

$^1/_2$ fresh red chilli
800g/1$^3/_4$lb tomatoes,
   peeled
$^1/_2$ cucumber, roughly
   sliced
1 red (bell) pepper,
   seeded and cut into
   chunks
1 celery stick, chopped
1 spring onion (scallion),
   roughly chopped
small handful of fresh
   coriander (cilantro),
   stalks included, plus
   extra to garnish
juice of 1 lime
salt
ice cubes

1 Using a sharp knife, seed the chilli. Add to a blender or food processor with the tomatoes, cucumber, red pepper, celery, spring onion and coriander.

2 Secure the lid of the blender or processor, then pulse the mixture. Blend until smooth, scraping the vegetable mixture down from the side of the bowl.

3 Add the lime juice and a little salt and blend. Pour into glasses. Add ice cubes and a few coriander leaves to serve.

Cook's tip
Stir in a little mineral water if the juice is still thick after blending. A splash of red wine vinegar will intensify the flavour.

Energy 32kcal/137kJ; Protein 1.5g; Carbohydrate 5.7g, of which sugars 5.6g; Fat 0.5g, of which saturates 0.2g; Cholesterol 0mg; Calcium 22mg; Fibre 1.9g; Sodium 19mg.

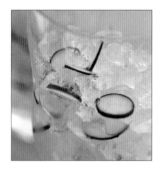

mixed salad soother

Despite a reputation as being full of water, lettuce and cucumber contain important minerals such as calcium and zinc, alongside other crucial nutrients like vitamin K. Spinach contains plenty of betacarotene and has cancer-fighting properties. Juice with ripe pears for maximum sweetness, and add radishes for a peppery accent note.

Makes 2–3 glasses

1/2 cucumber
1/2 cos or romaine lettuce
2 large, ripe pears
75g/3oz fresh spinach
6–8 radishes
crushed ice
sliced radishes and
    cucumber, to garnish

1 Using a small, sharp knife, chop the cucumber into chunks. Roughly tear the lettuce into pieces. Quarter the pears and remove the core.

2 Push all the ingredients, except the ice, through a juicer. Place the crushed ice in tall glasses, and pour the juice over the top. Serve with sliced radishes and cucumber swizzle sticks.

Cook's tip
Although it can taste fairly bland in a salad, unpeeled cucumber has a surprisingly intense flavour when it is juiced. If you prefer a lighter taste, peel the cucumber with a sharp knife before juicing.

Energy 64kcal/270kJ; Protein 2.1g; Carbohydrate 12.9g, of which sugars 12.8g; Fat 0.7g, of which saturates 0.1g; Cholesterol 0mg; Calcium 88mg; Fibre 3.9g; Sodium 44mg.

celery sensation

Savoury, almost salty, celery and sweet, green grapes make an astoundingly effective twosome when combined in a blended juice. A small handful of peppery watercress adds an extra punch, but be careful not to add too much because its flavour intensifies considerably when the leaves are juiced.

Makes 1 large glass

2 celery sticks
few celery leaves
a handful of watercress
200g/7oz/1¾ cups
   green grapes
1 leafy celery stick, to
   serve
crushed ice

1 With the aid of a plunger, push the celery sticks through a juicer, followed by the celery leaves, the watercress and the green grapes.

2 Half-fill each glass with the crushed ice, and put a leafy celery stick in each to act as an edible swizzle stick. Pour over the juice so that it just covers the ice, and serve immediately.

Health tip
Celery has one of the lowest calorie contents of all vegetables. The same cannot be said of the grapes, however, so enjoy this in moderation if you are on a low-calorie diet. Grapes are great detoxifiers.

Energy 135kcal/579kJ; Protein 2.6g; Carbohydrate 31.5g, of which sugars 31.5g; Fat 0.8g, of which saturates 0.1g; Cholesterol 0mg; Calcium 136mg; Fibre 2.8g; Sodium 65mg.

broccoli booster

Hailed as a cure-all superfood and a vital ingredient in a healthy diet, broccoli is packed with antiviral nutrients and contains almost as much calcium as milk. The vegetable's strong taste does, however, need a bit of toning down when the raw vegetable is juiced. Sweet and tangy apples and lemon juice soften its flavour.

Makes 1 tall glass

125g/4¼oz broccoli
    florets

2 eating apples
15ml/1 tbsp lemon
    juice
ice cubes

1 Using a sharp knife, trim any broccoli florets that have longer stalks, and cut each floret in half. Quarter the apples.

2 Push both through a juicer and stir in the lemon juice. Pour into a tall glass and serve with plenty of ice.

Cook's tip
Don't juice the tough broccoli stalks as they provide little juice and they don't have as good a flavour as the delicate florets.

Energy 111kcal/475kJ; Protein 6.1g; Carbohydrate 20.1g, of which sugars 19.7g; Fat 1.3g, of which saturates 0.3g; Cholesterol 0mg; Calcium 78mg; Fibre 6.5g; Sodium 14mg.

red alert

This juice is perfect for those times when you're not thinking straight or you need to concentrate. Beetroot, carrots and spinach all contain folic acid, which is known to help maintain a healthy brain, while the addition of fresh orange juice will give your body a natural vitamin boost. This delicious and vibrant blend is guaranteed to set your tastebuds tingling.

Makes 1 large or 2 small glasses

200g/7oz raw beetroot (beets)
1 carrot
1 large orange
50g/2oz spinach

Cook's tip
You should only use fresh, raw, firm beetroot for juicing, not the cooked variety – and most definitely avoid the type that is pickled in vinegar or packed in jars.

1 Using a sharp knife, cut the beetroot into wedges. Roughly chop the carrot, then cut away the skin from the orange and roughly slice the flesh.

2 Push the orange slices, beetroot wedges and carrot pieces through a juicer, then add the spinach. Pour into glasses and serve.

Energy 65kcal/273kJ; Protein 2.8g; Carbohydrate 13.2g, of which sugars 12.4g; Fat 0.5g, of which saturates 0.1g; Cholesterol 0mg; Calcium 75mg; Fibre 1.4g; Sodium 113mg.

avocado cleanser

Avocados are extremely good for the skin, mainly because of their high vitamin E content. Combined with parsley, asparagus and orange, this juice makes a great cleanser and skin tonic. If you have a particular skin problem, drinking this juice regularly should really make a difference – it is extremely effective and will benefit your overall health too.

Makes 2 glasses

1 small avocado
small handful of parsley
75g/3oz tender asparagus
   spears
2 large oranges
squeeze of lemon juice
ice cubes
mineral water
orange wedges, to
   decorate

Cook's tip
The orange and lemon juice in this blend means that the avocados will not discolour, so you might want to refrigerate a glass for later on. If the juice has thickened slightly, stir in a little extra mineral water.

1 Halve the avocado and discard the stone (pit). Scoop the flesh into a blender or food processor. Remove any tough stalks from the parsley and chop.

2 Roughly chop the asparagus and add to the avocado with the parsley stalks. Blend the mixture thoroughly until smooth, scraping down from the side of the bowl, if necessary.

3 Juice the oranges and, using a squeezer or reamer, add to the mixture with the lemon juice. Blend briefly until the mixture is very smooth.

4 Pour the juice into two glasses until two-thirds full, then add ice cubes and stir in a little mineral water to thin out. Garnish with chunky orange wedges.

Variation
Replace the asparagus with an apple, if you like. Apples are naturally cleansing and blood-purifying and are often recommended for helping with skin problems.

Energy 123kcal/507kJ; Protein 2.3g; Carbohydrate 6.1g, of which sugars 5.4g; Fat 10g, of which saturates 2.1g; Cholesterol 0mg; Calcium 21mg; Fibre 2.4g; Sodium 9mg.

sugar snap

Sweet sugar snap peas are one of the most delicious vegetables to serve raw and they taste just as good when put through a juicer. The sweetness of the peas is intensified by the melon, and the fresh root ginger adds a certain edge to this mellow, cooling blend. Keep the melon in the refrigerator so that it's well and truly chilled when you come to make the juice – you won't need to add ice.

Makes 1 large glass

1cm/^{1}/$_2$ in piece fresh
    root ginger, peeled
^{1}/$_4$ honeydew or Galia
    melon
200g/7oz sugar snap
    peas, including pods
melon chunks and peas,
    to decorate

1 Using a sharp knife, slice the ginger finely. Scoop out the seeds from the melon.

2 Cut the melon into wedges, then cut away the skin and discard it. Chop the melon flesh into chunks.

3 Push the sugar snap peas through a juicer, followed by the melon chunks and the slices of ginger.

4 Pack some melon chunks and peas into a large glass, pour over the juice and serve.

Cook's tips

• Use a fresh, plump-looking piece of ginger. If it is too old, it may have started to shrivel and won't yield the necessary juice; nor will it have much flavour.

• Root ginger freezes very well and is easy to peel when just starting to thaw. No preparation is necessary before freezing; just pop the clean root in a tub or plastic bag and store in the freezer.

Variation
Use peaches or nectarines instead of melon. These fruits also go very well with ginger.

Energy 112kcal/476kJ; Protein 8.2g; Carbohydrate 19.6g, of which sugars 18g; Fat 0.6g, of which saturates 0g; Cholesterol 0mg; Calcium 114mg; Fibre 5.4g; Sodium 66mg.

something
special

spicy bloody mary

This recipe has plenty of spicy character, with horseradish, sherry and Tabasco. Made with chilli or pepper vodka, it is a much hotter proposition than the standard recipe. For the best flavour, use really ripe organic tomatoes on the vine. This adults-only drink is ideal for a pick-me-up on an evening when you are staying in.

Makes 2 glasses

3 large ripe tomatoes,
    about 400g/14oz
75ml/3fl oz/6 tbsp chilli-
    flavoured vodka
45ml/3 tbsp sherry
    (preferably fino sherry)
25ml/1½ tbsp lemon
    juice

2–3 dashes Tabasco sauce
10–15ml/2–3 tsp
    Worcestershire sauce
2.5ml/½ tsp creamed
    horseradish
5ml/1 tsp celery salt
ground black pepper
celery stalk, stuffed green
    olives and a cherry
    tomato, to garnish

1 Cut the tomatoes in half and push them through a juicer. This should yield about 300ml/½ pint/ 1¼ cups juice.

2 Fill a pitcher with cracked ice and add the vodka, sherry and tomato juice. Stir well. Add the lemon juice, Tabasco, Worcestershire sauce and horseradish. Stir again.

3 Add the celery salt, salt and pepper, and stir until the pitcher has frosted and the contents are chilled. Strain into tumblers, half-filled with ice cubes. Add a stick of celery, preferably leafy; thread the olives and cherry tomato onto a cocktail stick (toothpick) and place across the top. Serve immediately.

Energy 149kcal/621kJ; Protein 1.6g; Carbohydrate 7.5g, of which sugars 7.5g; Fat 0.7g, of which saturates 0.2g; Cholesterol 0mg; Calcium 26mg; Fibre 2.1g; Sodium 583mg.

cinnamon squash

Lightly cooked butternut squash makes a delicious smoothie. It has a wonderfully rich, rounded flavour that is lifted perfectly by the addition of tart citrus juice and warm, spicy cinnamon. Imagine pumpkin pie as a gorgeous smooth drink and you're halfway to experiencing the flavours of this lusciously sweet and tantalizing treat.

Makes 2–3 small glasses

1 small butternut squash, about 600g/1lb 6oz
2.5ml/1/2 tsp ground cinnamon
3 large lemons
1 grapefruit
60ml/4 tbsp light muscovado (brown) sugar
ice cubes

1 Halve the squash, scoop out the seeds and cut the flesh into chunks.

2 Cut away the skin and discard. Steam or boil the squash for 10–15 minutes until just tender. Drain well and leave until cool enough to handle.

3 Put the cooled squash in a blender or food processor and add the ground cinnamon.

4 Squeeze the lemons and grapefruit and pour the juice over the squash, then add the muscovado sugar.

5 Process the ingredients until they are very smooth. If necessary, pause to scrape down the side of the food processor or blender.

6 Put a few ice cubes in two or three short glasses and pour over the smoothie. Serve immediately.

Energy 121kcal/513kJ; Protein 1.9g; Carbohydrate 28.9g, of which sugars 27.9g; Fat 0.5g, of which saturates 0.2g; Cholesterol 0mg; Calcium 81mg; Fibre 2.7g; Sodium 3mg.

red hot chilli pepper

Sweet red peppers make a colourful, light juice that's best mixed with other ingredients for a full flavour impact. Courgettes add a subtle, almost unnoticeable body to the drink, while chilli and radishes contribute a kick of peppery heat. Freshly squeezed orange juice adds sweetness as well as a good dose of vitamin C.

Makes 2–3 glasses

2 red (bell) peppers
1 fresh red chilli, seeded
150g/5oz courgettes
    (zucchini)
75g/3oz radishes
1 orange
ice cubes

Cook's tip

Buy radishes with a bright colour and firm texture, and keep refrigerated until using.

1 Halve the red peppers, remove the cores and seeds, quarter the pieces and push them through a juicer with the chilli.

2 Cut the courgettes into chunks, halve the radishes and push them through the juicer.

3 Cut the orange into halves and squeeze them. Pour into the vegetable juice and stir until thoroughly blended.

4 Fill two or three tall glasses with ice, pour over the juice and serve. Garnish with sliced pepper or a single fresh red chilli, if you like.

Cook's tip

When working with chillies, always wash your hands thoroughly with soap after chopping them. You should still avoid touching your eyes or any other delicate area directly afterwards because the capsacin in the chillies will make them sting. Alternatively, wear protective gloves when chopping chillies.

Energy 64kcal/269kJ; Protein 2.7g; Carbohydrate 12.2g, of which sugars 11.8g; Fat 0.8g, of which saturates 0.2g; Cholesterol 0mg; Calcium 45mg; Fibre 3.2g; Sodium 10mg.

Makes 4 small glasses

3 ripe avocados
juice of 1^1/$_2$ limes
1 garlic clove, crushed
a handful of ice cubes
400ml/14fl oz/1^2/$_3$ cups
  vegetable stock, chilled
400ml/14fl oz/1^2/$_3$ cups
  milk, chilled
150ml/^{1}/$_4$ pint/^{2}/$_3$ cup
  sour cream, chilled
a few drops of Tabasco
  sauce
salt and ground black
  pepper
fresh coriander (cilantro)
  leaves, to garnish
extra virgin olive oil, to
  serve

For the salsa

4 tomatoes, peeled,
  seeded and finely diced
2 spring onions
  (scallions), finely
  chopped
1 fresh green chilli,
  seeded and finely
  chopped
15ml/1 tbsp chopped
  fresh coriander
  (cilantro)
juice of ^{1}/$_2$ lime

avocado and lime blend

This lovely light drink is almost substantial enough to be served as a chilled soup, and is a perfect al fresco pleaser.

1 Prepare the salsa first. Mix the tomatoes, spring onions, chilli, coriander and lime juice in a bowl. Season well and chill.

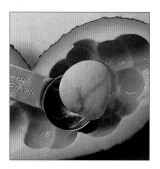

2 Halve and stone (pit) the avocados. Scoop the flesh out of the avocado skins and place in a food processor or blender. Add the lime juice, garlic, ice cubes and 150ml/^{1}/$_4$ pint/^{2}/$_3$ cup of the vegetable stock.

3 Process until smooth. Pour into a large bowl. Stir in the remaining stock, milk, sour cream, Tabasco and seasoning.

4 Ladle the avocado and lime blend into four chilled glasses and spoon a little salsa on top to garnish. Add a splash of olive oil to each portion and garnish with fresh coriander leaves. Serve immediately.

Cook's tips
• The avocados should be really ripe for this recipe. If they are still a little too firm, place them in a brown paper bag with a banana or apple and leave in a dark place for a couple of days. This hastens the process as the added fruits give off small amounts of the gas ethylene, which acts as a ripening agent.
• This blend may discolour if left standing for too long, but the flavour will not be spoilt. Give it a quick whisk just before serving.

Energy 335kcal1390kJ; Protein 7.3g; Carbohydrate 12g, of which sugars 10.6g; Fat 28.9g, of which saturates 10g; Cholesterol 28mg; Calcium 176mg; Fibre 4.7g; Sodium 76mg.

Tarragon, orange and sun-dried tomato juice

Fans of tomato juice are sure to get hooked on this flavour-packed, revitalizing blend. Fresh orange makes it irresistibly moreish and adds extra vitamin C, while tarragon contributes a lovely aromatic note. Add a dash of Tabasco or chilli sauce instead of the ground black pepper if you simply cannot resist the classic combination of chilli and tomato.

Makes 2 tall glasses

4 large sprigs of tarragon,
   plus extra to garnish
500g/1lb 2oz tomatoes
2 large oranges
15ml/1 tbsp sun-dried
   tomato paste
ice cubes
ground black pepper

Variations
• Sun-dried tomato paste gives this juice real depth of flavour, but regular tomato purée (paste) can be used instead.
• Alternatively, try adding a little harissa, a lovely, warm chilli paste from North Africa.

1 Pull the tarragon leaves from their stalks. Roughly chop the tomatoes.

2 Push the tomatoes through a juicer, alternating them with the tarragon leaves. It is not recommended that you juice the tarragon stalks.

3 Squeeze the juice from the oranges by hand or using a citrus juicer.

4 Stir the orange juice into the tomato mixture. Add the sun-dried tomato paste and stir well to mix all the ingredients together and to intensify colour and flavour.

5 Place ice cubes into two tall chilled glasses and pour over the juice. Add a light grinding of black pepper to taste, and a garnish of tarragon sprigs. Serve immediately with decorative stirrers, if you have them.

Energy 93kcal/397kJ; Protein 3.5g; Carbohydrate 19g, of which sugars 19g; Fat 0.9g, of which saturates 0.3g; Cholesterol 0mg; Calcium 77mg; Fibre 4.8g; Sodium 47mg.

green devil

Choose a well-flavoured avocado, such as a knobbly, dark-skinned Hass, for this slightly spicy, hot and sour smoothie. Cucumber adds a refreshing edge, while lemon and lime juice zip up the flavour, and the chilli sauce adds an irresistible fiery bite. This is one little devil that is sure to liven up even the most lethargic days.

Makes 2–3 glasses

1 small ripe avocado
1/2 cucumber
30ml/2 tbsp lemon juice
30ml/2 tbsp lime juice
10ml/2 tsp caster
   (superfine) sugar
pinch of salt
250ml/8fl oz/1 cup apple
   juice or mineral water
10–20ml/2–4 tsp sweet
   chilli sauce
ice cubes
red chilli curls, to garnish

1 Halve the avocado and use a sharp knife to remove the stone (pit). Scoop the flesh from both halves into a blender or food processor.

2 Peel and roughly chop the cucumber and add to the blender or food processor, then add the lemon and lime juice, the caster sugar and a little salt to taste.

3 Process the ingredients until smooth and creamy, then add the apple juice or mineral water and a little of the chilli sauce. Blend once more to lightly mix the ingredients together.

4 Pour the smoothie into glasses filled with ice cubes. Decorate with red chilli curls and serve with a dash of chilli sauce.

Cook's tip
To make chilli curls, core and seed a fresh red chilli then cut it into very fine strips. Put the strips in a bowl of iced water and leave to stand for 20 minutes or until the strips curl. Use them to decorate this smoothie.

Variation
Instead of using sweet chilli sauce, try adding Tabasco green pepper sauce. Much milder than the more familiar red variety, this is made from jalapeno chillies and gives the smoothie a rich, tangy taste.

Energy 143kcal/598kJ; Protein 1.3g; Carbohydrate 13.2g, of which sugars 12.5g; Fat 9.8g, of which saturates 2.1g; Cholesterol 0mg; Calcium 19mg; Fibre 1.9g; Sodium 6mg.

sunburst

Bursting with freshness and vitamins, this sunny fruit-and-vegetable blend makes a fantastic non-alcoholic cocktail. Serve it as soon as possible after making as the mixture may begin to separate if left to stand.

Makes 2 tall glasses

1 green apple, cored and chopped
3 carrots, chopped
1 mango, peeled and stoned (pitted)
150ml/1/4 pint/2/3 cup orange juice, chilled
6 strawberries, hulled
orange slices, to decorate

1 Place the apple, carrots and mango in a blender or food processor and process to make a smooth purée.

2 Add the orange juice and strawberries and process again.

3 Strain well through a sieve, pressing out all the juice with the back of a wooden spoon. Discard any pulp left in the sieve.

4 Pour into tumblers filled with ice cubes and serve immediately, decorated with a slice of orange on the side of the glass.

Energy 103kcal/438kJ; Protein 1.5g; Carbohydrate 24.9g, of which sugars 24.5g; Fat 0.4g, of which saturates 0.1g; Cholesterol 0mg; Calcium 32mg; Fibre 3.8g; Sodium 21mg.

cucumber, kiwi and stem ginger spritzer

The tangy flavour of kiwi fruit becomes sweeter and more intense when the flesh is juiced. Choose plump, unwrinkled fruits that yield to very gentle pressure, as under-ripe fruits will produce a slightly bitter taste.

Makes 1 tall glass

2 kiwi fruit
1/2 cucumber, peeled
1 piece preserved stem ginger, plus 15ml/1 tbsp syrup from the ginger jar
sparkling mineral water

1 Using a sharp knife, roughly chop the kiwi fruit. Cut the cucumber into large chunks. Chop the stem ginger.

2 Push the cucumber, ginger and kiwi fruit through a juicer and pour the juice into a jug (pitcher). Stir in the ginger syrup.

3 Pour the juice into a tall glass, then top up with sparkling mineral water and serve immediately.

Energy 114kcal/479kJ; Protein 2.1g; Carbohydrate 26.1g, of which sugars 25.6g; Fat 0.7g, of which saturates 0g; Cholesterol 0mg; Calcium 50mg; Fibre 2.9g; Sodium 48mg.

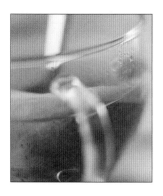

chamomile and leaf tonic

Some herbal teas are known for their purely soporific qualities, but this concoction is slightly more substantial. It is just what you need when you want to relax.

Makes 1 large glass

1 chamomile teabag
90g/3½oz iceberg lettuce
1 small banana
juice of ½ lemon

1 Put the teabag in a jug (pitcher) and pour over 150ml/¼ pint/⅔ cup boiling water. Leave to steep for 10 minutes.

2 Chop the lettuce into large pieces. When the tea has steeped and acquired plenty of flavour, drain the teabag.

3 Chop the banana into a blender or food processor, add the lettuce and blend well until smooth, scraping the mixture down from the sides of the bowl, if necessary.

4 Add the lemon juice and chamomile tea and blend until smooth. Serve immediately.

Cook's tip
If you have chamomile growing in the garden, gather the flowers as soon as they appear. Use three or four flower-heads instead of the chamomile teabag. Steep them in the boiling water for a few minutes, but don't leave them for too long or the flavour will be bitter.

Variation
For a calming, and slightly lighter daytime herbal tea, substitute the banana with some ripe mango.

Health tip
Bananas provide slow-release carbohydrates to ward off hunger through the night and lettuce is renowned for its sleep-inducing properties.

Energy 89kcal/376kJ; Protein 1.7g; Carbohydrate 20.1g, of which sugars 18.3g; Fat 0.7g, of which saturates 0.2g; Cholesterol 0mg; Calcium 30mg; Fibre 1.7g; Sodium 4mg.

index